Christmas '07

My dear Char –
You know I love books, &
you should love this too! Really
though, the pictures are wonderful –
so lovely & peaceful. Cherish each
picture & relax in time and let it
take you to another wonderful time
in history. I love you & cherish
you beyond words!!
Merry Christmas honey –
love,
mom :)

Celebrate the Gift

A CHRISTMAS TREASURY
FROM *Focus on the Family*

Paintings by SANDRA KUCK

HARVEST HOUSE PUBLISHERS
Eugene, Oregon

Celebrate the Gift

Text Copyright © 2000 by Focus on the Family®
Published by Harvest House Publishers
Eugene, Oregon 97402

Focus on the Family, headed by Dr. James Dobson, is an organization that reaches families with the message of God's love. Focus on the Family® is a registered trademark of Focus on the Family, Colorado Springs, CO 80995. For more information, please contact:

> Focus on the Family
> Colorado Springs, CO 80995
> 1-800-A-Family
> www.family.org

Library of Congress Cataloging-in-Publication Data
Kuck, Sandra, 1947-
  Celebrate the gift : a Christmas treasury from Focus on the Family / paintings by
Sandra Kuck.
   p. cm.
  ISBN 0-7369-0282-1
   1. Christmas—United States. 2. Family life—United States. 3. United States—Social life and customs.
  I. Title.
  GT4986.A1 K83 2000
  394.2663'0973—dc21

00-035116

All works of art in this book are copyrighted by Sandra Kuck and may not be reproduced without permission. For information regarding art in this book, please contact:

> V.E. Fine Arts, Inc.
> 11191 Westheimer, #202
> Houston, TX 77042

Design and production by Garborg Design Works, Minneapolis, MN

Harvest House Publishers has made every effort to trace the ownership of all poems and quotes. In the event of a question arising from the use of a poem or quote, we regret any error made and will be pleased to make the necessary correction in future editions of this book.

Special thanks to all those who allowed us to share their Christmas stories.

"Christmas Far from Home," copyright © by Roberta Donovan. Used by permission.
"The Centerpiece," copyright © by Bob Welch. Used by permission.
"A Visit from the Christ Child," copyright © 1986 by F.R. Duplantier. Used by permission.
"A Brighter Vision of Christmas," copyright © by Gary Swanson. Used by permission.
"A Symbol of Faith," copyright © by Emilie Barnhardt. Used by permission.
"A Giving Spirit," copyright © by Bonnie Shepherd. Used by permission.

Scripture quotations are taken from the Holy Bible, New International Version®, Copyright © 1973, 1978, 1984 by the International Bible Society. Used by permission of Zondervan Publishing House.

Printed in the United States of America

00 01 02 03 04 05 06 07 08 09 /IP/ 10 9 8 7 6 5 4 3 2

Contents

Somehow not only for Christmas

but all the long year through,

The joy that you give others

is the joy that comes back to you.

JOHN GREENLEAF WHITTIER

The Shirt Off My Back

As we stood gazing at the flood damage, God's compassion stirred us for the people who had lost their homes, their belongings, and, for some, their loved ones.

We had come to Mexico to help the people. Packed into our vehicles were blankets, warm clothing, large cauldrons of hot soup, medicine, money, shoes, and most of all, the hope that God can bring.

We began working in groups. One group dispensing medications and consulting the sick. Another group fitting children with shoes. Another group giving away blankets, food, clothing, and whatever else was there. We worked all day and were exhausted but content.

As the sun began to set, an elderly man unexpectedly appeared before me. He had on a pair of jeans and a soiled T-shirt. He was barefoot. As he stood shivering in the mud, he asked, "No tienes algo para mi?" (Don't you have anything for me?)

I had nothing left! The old man searched my face for hope, and as I looked down at the ground it dawned on me that I was wearing a wool Pendleton shirt. I shed the shirt and slipped it on the man, buttoning it up and smiling big at him. He beamed back at me, cupping his hands together. As his eyes locked with mine, I felt an overpowering love for him.

Two months later on Christmas morning, we were huddled around the Christmas tree when an aunt from back east handed me a gift. I opened it, and, to my amazement, there before me was a brand-new Pendleton, the same color I had given away. I started laughing and had to explain to the group what had happened down in Mexico.

That night, as I thought about the day, a verse in Proverbs came to me: "He that hath pity upon the poor lendeth unto the Lord, and that which he hath given will he pay him again." This truth became a living reality for me that Christmas morning.

WARREN BISSELL

One doesn't forget the rounded

wonder in the eyes of a boy as he

comes bursting upstairs on

Christmas morning and finds the

two-wheeler or fire truck of which

for weeks he scarcely dared dream.

MAX LERNER

Christmas may be many things

or it may be a few:

For you, the joy

is each new toy;

for me, it's watching you.

Sleep well
little children
wherever you are;
Tomorrow is Christmas
beneath every star
Soon the snowflakes will fall
and tomorrow you'll see
Every wish
one and all
waiting under the tree.
Sleep well
little children
pleasant dreams through the night;
Tomorrow is Christmas
all merry and bright
Soon you'll hear the bells ring
time for dreams to come true
As the world wakes to bring
Merry Christmas to you.

A. BERGMAN AND L. KLATZKIN

Santa Exposed!

Every Christmas Eve my parents would encourage us to set out milk and cookies for Santa, to thank him for the presents he brought us. I remember one Christmas Eve more clearly than others.

I was five years old and very interested about who this Santa was and what he actually looked like. The evening started just like any other Christmas Eve, with the setting out of the milk and cookies. But in my mind these items were not for thanking Santa but instead were to be used as bait. I was going to find out exactly who this Santa was.

I went to bed anxious about my plan, for I knew that when I heard movement I must be quick to act. Around 12:30 it happened—the noise I had been waiting for! Quietly I crept out of my bed and crawled down the hallway. Excitedly, I poked my head around the corner, hoping to glimpse the man responsible for so much Christmas joy. As I turned the corner, my hopes were realized but not in the manner I had expected. There, at the table, sat my father finishing off the last of the Christmas cookies and milk. As he wiped his mouth, he spied me looking around the corner in disbelief. As the smile touched his eyes, he responded only with the words, "Ho, Ho, Ho!"

I found out that year that Santa dwells in the hearts of loving parents who, with a selfless attitude, give a mythical being the credit for their good deeds for the single purpose of increasing their children's joy. Thanks, Mom and Dad.

JEFF L. JORGENSEN

The most splendid Christmas gift,

the most marveled and magic,

is the gift that has not yet been opened.

Opaque behind wrapping or winking foil,

is a box full of possibilities.

GEORGE EASTERBROOK

The Wisdom of Time

I will never forget the Christmas when I was ten years old. My dear mom wanted badly to give something special to my dad, my brother, and me. She did extra sewing and saved her loose change in order to purchase this special gift.

On that Christmas morning, we went to my older brother's house (he was already married with a small child) just across the field from our home to watch their little one open her gifts.

Mom had three envelopes she put on their tree for us (Dad, my brother, and me) to receive while we were there. She was a very thrifty lady and wise beyond her years. When we were given our envelopes, we were surprised to say the least, for in each envelope she had specific instructions for each of us to follow.

When we left my brother's house, each of us had a "chore" to do and then report to another place to receive "what we were working for." Needless to say, we hastened to do the chore we were assigned, then rushed to the place that each of us had been instructed, only

to find another "chore" to do, then report to yet another place. Of course we did what was asked, wondering, *When is this going to end?*

We were beginning to realize that Mom had outwitted us and was getting the chores done that needed doing before we were to be rewarded. She got the pets fed, the beds made, the dishes washed, porches swept, rugs shook out, and I'm sure more that has escaped my memory. But each of us gladly did what was assigned in order to get our most coveted prize. *Surely it has to be good*, we thought, and, you know, it was!

I was to report to the left top sewing machine drawer to find my treasure. My brother had to report to the bread box in the kitchen, my dad to his sock drawer in their bedroom dresser. We were instructed to report to one last place at the same time, and, oh, the surprise and delight when we opened our prizes! We each had a new watch. It was my first!

I cherished that watch, and I still have it forty-seven years later. Now that I have been through the joys of rearing children, I realize the sacrifice that my sweet mom made for us in order to give us such a special gift. My mom and dad are now in heaven, but that memory will forever be a treasure to me.

PHYLLIS ELLIS

May no gift be too small to give, nor too simple to receive, which is wrapped in thoughtfulness, and tied with love.

L.O. BAIRD

Silent night, holy night,

All is calm, all is bright.

*Round yon Virgin,
Mother and Child!*

*Holy Infant so tender
and mild,*

Sleep in heavenly peace,

Sleep in heavenly peace.

JOSEPH MOHR
"Silent Night"

A Brighter Vision of Christmas

The mother sat on the simulated-leather chair in the doctor's office, picking nervously at her fingernails. Wrinkles of worry lined her forehead as she watched five-year-old Kenny sitting on the rug before her.

He is small for his age and a little too thin, she thought. His fine blond hair hung down smooth and straight to the top of his ears. But white gauze bandages encircled his head, covering his eyes and pinning his ears back.

In his lap he bounced a beaten-up teddy bear. It was the pride of his life, yet one arm was gone and one eye was missing. Twice his mother had tried to throw the bear away, to replace it with a new one, but he had fussed so much she had relented. She tipped her head slightly to the side and smiled at him. *It's really about all he has*, she sighed to herself.

A nurse appeared in the doorway. "Kenny Ellis," she announced, and the young mother scooped up the boy and followed the nurse toward the examination room. The hallway smelled of rubbing alcohol and bandages. Children's crayon drawings lined the walls.

"The doctor will be with you in a moment," the nurse said with an efficient smile. "Please be seated."

The mother placed Kenny on the examination table. "Be careful, Honey, not to fall off."

"Am I up very high, Mother?"

"No, dear, but be careful."

Kenny hugged his teddy bear tighter. "Then I don't want Grr-face to fall either."

The mother smiled. The smile twisted at the corners into a frown of concern. She brushed the hair out of the boy's face and caressed his cheek, soft as thistledown, with the back of her hand. As the office music drifted into a haunting version of "Silent Night," she remembered the accident for the thousandth time.

She had been cooking things on the back burners for years. But there it was, sitting right out in front, the water almost boiling for oatmeal.

The phone rang in the living room. It was another one of those "free offers" that cost so much. At the very moment she returned the phone to the table, Kenny screamed in the kitchen, the galvanizing cry of pain that frosts a mother's veins.

She winced again at the memory of it and brushed aside a warm tear slipping down her cheek. Six weeks they had waited for this day to come. "We'll be able to take the bandages off the week before Christmas," the doctor had said.

The door to the examination room swept open, and Dr. Harris came in. "Good morning, Mrs. Ellis," he said brightly. "How are you today?"

"Fine, thank you," she said. But she was too apprehensive for small talk.

Dr. Harris bent over the sink and washed his hands carefully. He was cautious with his patients but careless about himself. He could seldom find time to get a haircut, and his straight black hair hung a little long over his collar. His loosed tie allowed his collar to be open at the throat.

"Now then," he said, sitting down on a stool, "let's have a look."

Gently he snipped at the bandage with scissors and unwound it from Kenny's head. The bandage fell away, leaving two flat squares of gauze taped directly over Kenny's eyes. Dr. Harris lifted the edges of the tape slowly, trying not to hurt the boy's tender skin.

Kenny slowly opened his eyes, blinked several times as if the sudden light hurt. Then he looked at his mother and grinned. "Hi, Mom," he said.

Choking and speechless, the mother threw her arms around Kenny's neck. For several minutes she could say nothing as she hugged the boy and wept in thankfulness. Finally, she looked at Dr. Harris with tear-filled eyes. "I don't know how we'll ever be able to pay you," she said.

"We've been over all that before," the doctor interrupted with the wave of his hand. "I know how things are for you and Kenny. I'm glad I could help."

The mother dabbed at her eyes with a

well-used handkerchief, stood up, and took Kenny's hand. But just as she turned toward the door, Kenny pulled away and stood for a long moment looking uncertainly at the doctor. Then he held his teddy bear up by its one arm to the doctor.

"Here," he said, "take my Grr-face. He ought to be worth a lot of money."

Dr. Harris quietly took the broken bear in his two hands. "Thank you, Kenny. This will more than pay for my services."

The last few days before Christmas were especially good for Kenny and his mother. They sat together in the long evenings, watching the Christmas tree lights twinkle on and off. Bandages had covered Kenny's eyes for six weeks, so he seemed reluctant to close them in sleep. The fire dancing in the fireplace, the snowflakes sticking to his bedroom windows, the two small packages under the tree—all the lights and colors of the holiday fascinated him.

And then, on Christmas Eve, Kenny's mother answered the doorbell. No one was there, but a large box was on the porch, wrapped in shiny gold paper with a broad red ribbon and bow. A tag attached to the bow identified the box as intended for Kenny Ellis.

With a grin, Kenny tore the ribbon off the box, lifted the lid, and pulled out a teddy bear—his beloved Grr-face. Only now it had a new arm of brown corduroy and two new button eyes that glittered in the soft Christmas light. Kenny didn't seem to mind that the new arm did not match the other one. He just hugged his teddy bear and laughed.

Among the tissue in the box, the mother found a card. "Dear Kenny," it read. "I can sometimes help put boys and girls back together, but Mrs. Harris had to help me repair Grr-face. She's a better bear doctor than I am. Merry Christmas! Dr. Harris."

"Look, Mother," Kenny smiled, pointing to the button eyes. "Grr-face can see again—just like me!"

GARY SWANSON

How silently, how silently,

the wondrous gift is given!

So God imparts to human hearts

the blessings of His heaven.

No ear may hear His coming,

but in this world of sin,

Where meek souls will receive Him still,

the dear Christ enters in.

PHILLIP BROOKS
"O Little Town of Bethlehem"

*Year after
year, everyone
who came
brought a
gift...*

THE BOOK OF 2 CHRONICLES

All I Want for Christmas...

I underwent surgery for a brain tumor at the age of 3 and came home on Thanksgiving Day due to God miraculously healing me. The medical bills overwhelmed my parents and four brothers. They all had surrendered to the fact that at least we'd be together as a family for Christmas, even if we didn't have the presents and decorations as usual.

The night before Christmas, when saying my good-night prayer, I said to God, "Please, can I have a Christmas tree." I didn't ask, "Please, may I" or anything proper. I said "Please, can I have..."

My mom and dad both felt miserable that they couldn't even afford socks for me and my brothers, let alone a Christmas tree. My prayer weighed heavily on their minds. Little did they know that God was already on the job. That evening the youth group from our local church came knocking at our door when they knew we five boys would be asleep. They came bringing a Christmas tree, clothes, and food for our Christmas dinner.

I awoke with excitement over God's answer to my childlike faith. Then I said, "But God forgot the plug," for the tree was not yet decorated. Nevertheless, this is but one of the many glorious ways God has made Himself evident in my life.

DAVID J. TOOLEY

O Christmas tree, O Christmas tree,
Much pleasure doth thou bring me!
O Christmas tree, O Christmas tree,
Much pleasure doth thou bring me!
For every year the Christmas tree,
Brings to us all both joy and glee.
O Christmas tree, O Christmas tree,
Much pleasure doth thou bring me!

AUGUST ZARNACK

Beth played her gayest march, Amy threw open the door, and Meg enacted escort with great dignity. Mrs. March was both surprised and touched, and smiled with her eyes full as she examined her presents and read the little notes which accompanied them…There was a good deal of laughing and kissing and explaining, in the simple, loving fashion which makes these home festivals so pleasant at the time, so sweet to remember long afterward…

LOUISA MAY ALCOTT
Little Women

Going Nuts at Christmas

The week before Christmas, my eleven-year-old daughter Bonnie and my wife make lots of Christmas cookies. On Christmas Day we distribute them on festive paper plates. Then we add a few ordinary walnuts and one or two "trick nuts" for our "special" friends. Trick nuts are walnuts that the kids have carefully cracked open, replaced the contents with silly treats, and glued the shell back together again.

On Christmas Day we launch out, delivering them with a cheerful "Merry Christmas" to our neighbors and friends. We then hop in the van and take the last ones to our seniors and youth pastors.

Although we do this for the joy of giving, sometimes people anticipate our visit and greet us with a small gift. One year an elderly widow invited us in for some homemade Dutch pastries. Last year another neighbor gave us a large tin of popcorn. (This fall at her husband's funeral, she introduced me to someone as "the guy who brings Christmas cookies.")

For several weeks into January the stories dribble back about people's surprise in cracking open a nut and finding Hershey's Kisses and funny notes inside! It's a simple act, but it keeps the spirit of giving alive in our family each year.

TOM AND SUE COOPER

*God's gifts put
man's best dreams
to shame.*

ELIZABETH BARRETT BROWNING

A Christmas Baptism

As if in quiet awe and amazement, the silhouette of the elfish figure stood outside my classroom door, somewhat hesitant this day to enter as if the presence of the twinkling blue spruce made it necessary for him to have an invitation to enter.

"Good morning, Will."

"Hi, Mrs. Miller," the small voice replied.

"Will, would you please do me a favor? Could you take this watering can, fill it, and then water the tree? I was in such a hurry to get it set up before the start of school that I totally forgot about watering it."

His face beamed. His small stature straightened up, shoulders back and seemingly much taller. He announced that he knew just what to do. "Christmas trees need extra cold water," he said authoritatively, "and I know just where to get some."

His voice trailed off as he darted out the door and down the hall. As I began correcting a set of papers, a tiny voice said, "Here it is, Mrs. Miller. It's real cold. I know where there is a drinking fountain with extra special cold water."

As Will finished talking, I at last looked up from my desk to see him on his tippy toes proceeding to water the tree and all the paper ornaments from the very top.

Oh, my gosh! I thought. *How can I possibly stop him before he destroys the children's decorations without hurting his feelings or embarrassing him?*

As I began to speak, trusting the right words would come, I heard myself say calmly, "Perhaps you could pour that water into the tree stand."

"But how will the water get to the top?" he asked, quite dismayed.

I replied, "Trees are able to suck the water up their trunk and into their branches."

Not at all convinced, he asked skeptically, "Do you really think so?"

"Yes," I assured him.

In full faith Will poured the remaining water into the stand. And so, through the baptism of this lovely spruce tree and the precious innocence of a child, the Holy Spirit began to work God's plan for both of us that day by giving Will a special place in my heart.

Little did either of us know that two years later Will would be abandoned by his parents on the streets and that the Christmas tree memory would send me before a judge to become his foster mom.

NANCY MILLER

'Twas the morning of Christmas, when all through the house
All the family was frantic, including my spouse;
For each one of them had one thing only in mind,
To examine the presents St. Nick left behind.

The boxes and wrapping and ribbons and toys
Were strewn on the floor, and the volume of noise
Increased as our children began a big fight
Over who got the video games, who got the bike.

I looked at my watch and I said, slightly nervous,
"Let's get ready for church, so we won't miss the service."
The children protested, "We don't want to pray:
We've just got our presents, and we want to play!"

It dawned on me then that we had gone astray,
In confusing the purpose of this special day;
Our presents were many and very high-priced
But something was missing—that something was Christ!

I said, "Put the gifts down and let's gather together,
And I'll tell you a tale of the greatest gift ever."
A savior was promised when Adam first sinned,
And the hopes of the world upon Jesus were pinned.

"Abraham begat Isaac, who Jacob begat,
And through David the line went to Joseph, whereat
This carpenter married a maiden with child,
Who yet was a virgin, in no way defiled.

"Saying 'Hail, full of Grace,' an archangel appeared
To Mary the Blessed, among women revered:
The Lord willed she would bear—through the Spirit—a son.
Said Mary to Gabriel, 'God's will be done.'

"Now Caesar commanded a tax would be paid,
And all would go home while the census was made;
Thus Joseph and Mary did leave Galilee
For the city of David to pay this new fee.

"Mary's time had arrived, but the inn had no room,
So she laid in a manger the fruit of her womb;
And both Joseph and Mary admired as He napped
The Light of the World in His swaddling clothes wrapped.

"Three wise men from the East had come looking for news
Of the birth of the Savior, the King of the Jews;
They carried great gifts as they followed a star—
Gold, frankincense, myrrh, which they'd brought from afar.

"As the shepherds watched over their flocks on that night,
The glory of God shone upon them quite bright,
And an angel explained the intent of the birth,
Saying, 'Glory to God and His peace to the earth.'

"For this was the Messiah whom prophets foretold,
A good shepherd to bring His sheep back to the fold;
He was God become man, He would die on the cross,
He would rise from the dead to restore Adam's loss.

"Santa Claus, Christmas presents, a brightly lit pine,
Candy canes and spiked eggnog are all very fine;
Let's have fun celebrating, but leave not a doubt
That Christ is what Christmas is really about!"

The children right then put an end to the noise,
They dressed quickly for church, put away all their toys;
For they knew Jesus loved them and said they were glad
That He'd died for their sins, and to save their dear Dad.

PÈRE ROBÉRT
"A Visit from the Christ Child"

December gifts—custom, ceremony, celebration, consecration—come to us wrapped up, not in tissue and ribbons, but in cherished memories.

SARAH BAN BREATHNACH
Simple Abundance

The off'rings of the Eastern kings of old
Unto our Lord were incense, myrrh and gold;
Incense because a God; gold as a king;
And myrrh as to a dying man they bring.
Instead of incense (blessed Lord) if we
Can send a sigh or fervent prayer to thee,
Instead of myrrh if we can but provide
Tears that from penitential eyes do slide,
And though we have no gold; if for our part
We can present thee with a broken heart
Thou wilt accept: and say those Eastern kings
Did not present thee with more precious things.

NATHANIEL WANLEY
"Royal Presents"

Christmas Far from Home

As I gathered the diapers from the clothesline, the wind-driven snow stung my cheeks with icy particles that felt like tiny slivers of glass. I glanced over at the nearby shack where a family of five, soon to be six, lived in two small rooms. The wind was tearing at the tar-paper siding on their home and blowing the smoke from the stovepipe in a horizontal plume. I wondered if they were managing to stay warm.

It was not yet Christmas, but already my first winter in this "Southern" state of Arkansas seemed colder than what I had known back home in Montana. I hurried inside with my armload of laundry. The tiny heating stove in the living room glowed with warmth. I hovered over it, rubbing my fingers to warm them. But to be honest, the raw winter weather was only a small part of what was troubling me. My real ailment was homesickness. I brushed away a tear with the sleeve of my sweater. What was I doing here, so far from home?

The United States was barely into its second year of World War II. My husband was serving his country here at Blytheville Air Station, one of several air bases that had mushroomed up from the cotton fields of the Mississippi Valley. Like many other young wives, I had followed my serviceman to be where he was stationed.

It had seemed both patriotic and romantic when I boarded the train in my hometown of Lewistown, Montana, where our month-old son, Jimmy, had been born. But now, far from home and lonely, I didn't feel romantic.

I hated this barren little house, one with so few conveniences. There weren't even any curtains on the windows. The night before, while preparing supper, I had found a nest of baby mice in a back corner of the kitchen cupboard. My scream was probably heard all the way back to Big Sky country.

As I started folding Jimmy's diapers, I glanced at the scrawny little Christmas tree standing in the corner. I had at least made an effort to have a "normal" holiday, but my husband's paycheck didn't stretch far enough to buy more than a single string of lights for the tree. Their bright reds and blues blinked at me from among the strings of popcorn and paper chains I had made to trim the tree.

It was the approach of Christmas that had brought on my wave of homesickness. How could I feel the joyous spirit of Christmas so far away from my family and friends?

I remembered other Christmases when I was secure in the haven of my parents' home. If I closed my eyes, I could almost see the huge tree that reached all the way to the ceiling, presents piled high around it. I remembered the red and green "ropes" looped from the chandelier to the four corners of the room and the pleated red-tissue bell that hung in the archway. I smelled the sweet aroma of gingerbread men baking in the big kitchen range, the spicy aroma of mincemeat pies. In my mind, I could even hear the joyous carols echoing all the way to the back of the church as I sang in the choir. And I saw the crèche near the altar, surrounded by fragrant pine boughs.

A knock at the door interrupted my reverie. It was almost dark, and I wondered who it could be. As I opened the door, I immediately recognized the three small daughters who lived in the tar-paper shack behind my house. Sometimes our paths would cross when we fetched water from a common spigot in the backyard or made our way to the outhouse near the alley.

"Please, ma'am," the eldest girl began, "may we come in and look at your Christmas tree? We saw the pretty lights through the window."

As they trooped inside, an appreciative "ooh" went up simultaneously. The eldest squeezed her little sister's hand and whispered, "Isn't it beautiful?"

Only moments before, that tree had seemed so scrawny and inadequate. Now it took on a new dignity, a new beauty. I was sure these little tykes didn't have a Christmas tree in their home.

"It is pretty, isn't it," I said, pulling the youngest girl onto my lap. I could feel her little shoulder blades through her thin jacket, and noticed that her small hands were red with cold. I held them in my own hands to warm them.

"How would you children like some hot chocolate?" I asked. Their faces lit up in response, but the eldest reminded her sisters, "We can't stay long. Remember what Ma said."

Jimmy woke up while the girls were sipping their chocolate. They gathered around his crib to admire him. I thought of how the shepherds, their faces also shining with awe, had gathered around another Babe so long ago.

After they left, I rocked Jimmy and thought about the girls and their parents. Their father had a disabling lung condition and couldn't work. Their mother had very limited vision. She received a small "blind pension," which was all the family had to live on. On alternate days, the mother cooked either a pot of beans or a pot of cabbage on their two-burner kerosene stove. The steam from the bubbling pot provided warmth, and its contents was often all they had to eat. Once I had fixed a big kettle of stew and taken it over on the pretext that my husband didn't like it. I knew the children often went to bed hungry.

By the next morning, I had reached a decision. My destitute neighbors would not go hungry on Christmas Day if I could help it. Bundling Jimmy up in warm clothes, I went from house to house in the neighborhood, asking people I had not met before to contribute to a food basket for our needy neighbors.

As often happens when folks are made aware of a need, they responded generously. Not only was there enough food for a fine Christmas dinner, but there was also enough to make nourishing meals for several weeks to come.

But I kept remembering that tiny cold hand I had cradled in my own. With some of the money I had saved to spend on gifts for Jimmy and my husband, I bought three pairs of bright warm mittens. And then, in a wave of generosity, I also purchased three coloring books and a box of crayons.

It was while I was selecting coloring books that I overheard two women talking about a Christmas program that night at a nearby church. I had been in Arkansas for only six weeks, and I hadn't found a church home yet. Suddenly, this was something I wanted very much to do—go to church.

That night at supper, I asked my husband to attend the Christmas program with me. He agreed. As I washed the dishes, I glanced out the window and saw the dim light of a kerosene lamp shining from the window of my neighbors' small home. *I've done all I can to help them have a merry Christmas,* I thought. Or had I? What was the greatest gift I could give those three little girls? Wasn't it an opportunity to learn the true meaning of Christmas? The parents seemed pleased when I asked if the girls could go to the program with us. Inwardly, I rejoiced, because I was sure they had no religious training at all.

As we entered the beautifully decorated church, the children's eyes grew wide with wonder. They watched, totally enthralled, as the Sunday school students re-enacted the story of Christ's birth.

Walking home in the crisp night air, a small mittened hand in my own, I looked up at the stars twinkling in the black sky. Tears of joy welled up in my eyes as I realized that I was really celebrating Christmas. It didn't matter that I was far from home, or that I wouldn't be seeing family or friends. It didn't matter that my future looked uncertain in the midst of a world war.

I learned that it didn't matter where I celebrated Christmas. What mattered was that God's peace and love were real, and they filled my heart.

ROBERTA DONOVAN

In the Christmas times of long ago,
There was one event we used to know
That was better than any other;
It wasn't the toys that we hoped to get,
But the talks we had—and I hear them yet—
Of the gift we'd buy for Mother.

If ever love fashioned a Christmas gift,
Or saved its money and practiced thrift,
'Twas done in those days, my brother—
Those golden times of Long Gone By,
Of our happiest years, when you and I
Talked over the gift for Mother.

We hadn't gone forth on our different ways
Nor coined our lives into yesterdays
In the fires that smelt and smother,
And we whispered and planned in our youthful glee
Of that marvelous "something" which was to be
The gift of our hearts to Mother.

It had to be all that our purse could give,
Something she'd treasure while she could live
And better than any other.
We gave it the best of our love and thought,
And, Oh, the joy when at last we bought
That marvelous gift for Mother!

Now I think as we go on our different ways,
Of the joy of those vanished yesterdays.
How good it would be, my brother,
If this Christmastime we could only know
That same sweet thrill of the Long Ago
When we shared in the gift for Mother.

EDGAR GUEST
"The Christmas Gift for Mother"

It is possible to give without loving, but it is impossible to love without giving.

RICHARD BRAUNSTEIN

A Gift Packed with Punch

Even as a little girl growing up in Louisiana, I knew Christmas was a time for giving. That was why I just had to find a special present for Mother. After all, I was her only child, and since Daddy had died suddenly of a heart attack, there was no one to give her a present on Christmas morning.

Life had become harder since Daddy died. Even with Mother working, her income barely covered our expenses. She deserved something special!

For months I had been saving my allowance of 25 cents a week for the perfect present. One day I heard her mention how she had always wanted a punch bowl. I had no idea how much a punch bowl would cost. One night, Mother and I went to a big department store. While Mother hurried to the fabric section, a glass showcase caught my eye. Punch bowls! I had never noticed them there before.

Quickly I asked the salesman the price of each. To my amazement, one punch bowl with 12 tiny cups came to $11 plus tax. I had almost $12—just enough to buy it! The salesman gift wrapped it for me at no charge. Because the box was large and heavy, he called a porter to carry it to our car. Mother could not imagine what I had bought!

I don't remember what I got that Christmas, but I will never forget Mother's face that morning as she lifted up the beautiful crystal punch bowl. I remember it afresh every year when I make wassail and use that very punch bowl.

LINDA KIMBLE

Of all the dear sights in the world,
nothing is so beautiful
as a child when it is giving something.

MARGARET LEE RUNBECK

If I had the gift of expressing

The wish that I hope would come true,

Your Christmas would be even fairer

Than the fairness suggested by you.

AUTHOR UNKNOWN

"A merry Christmas, Bob!" said Scrooge, with an earnestness that could not be mistaken, as he clapped him on the back. "A merrier Christmas, Bob, my good fellow, than I have given you for many a year! I'll raise your salary, and endeavour to assist your struggling family, and we will discuss your affairs this very afternoon, over a Christmas bowl of smoking bishop, Bob! Make up the fires, and buy another coal-scuttle before you dot another i, Bob Cratchit."

Scrooge was better than his word. He did it all, and infinitely more; and to Tiny Tim, who did not die, he was a second father. He became as good a friend, as good a master, and as good a man, as the good old city knew, or any other good old city, town, or borough, in the good old world. Some people laughed to see the alteration in him, but he let them laugh, and little heeded them; for he was wise enough to know that nothing ever happened on this globe, for good, at which some people did not have their fill of laughter in the outset; and knowing that such as these would be blind anyway, he thought it quite as well that they should wrinkle up their eyes in grins, as have the malady in less attractive forms. His own heart laughed: and that was quite enough for him.

He had no further intercourse with Spirits, but lived upon the Total Abstinence Principle, ever afterwards; and it was always said of him, that he knew how to keep Christmas well, if any man alive possessed the knowledge. May that be truly said of us, and all of us! And so, as Tiny Tim observed, God Bless Us, Every One!

CHARLES DICKENS
A Christmas Carol

A Giving Spirit

With only two weeks before Christmas, the last place I wanted to be was in the hospital recovering from surgery. This was our family's first Christmas in Minnesota, and I wanted it to be memorable, but not this way.

For weeks I had been ignoring the pain in my left side, but when it got worse, I saw the doctor. "Gallstones," he said, peering at the X-rays. "Enough to string a necklace. You'll need surgery right away."

Despite my protests that this was a terrible time to be in the hospital, the gnawing pain in my side convinced me to go ahead with surgery. My husband, Buster, assured me he could take care of things at home, and I called a few friends for help with carpooling. A thousand other things—Christmas baking, shopping, and decorating—would have to wait.

I struggled to open my eyes after sleeping for the better part of two days in the hospital following my surgery. As I became more alert,

I looked around to what seemed like a Christmas floral shop. Red poinsettias and other bouquets crowded the windowsill. A stack of cards waited to be opened. On the stand next to my bed stood a small tree decorated with ornaments my children had made. The shelf over the sink held a dozen red roses from my parents in Indiana and a Yule log with candles from our neighbor. I was overwhelmed with all the love and attention.

Maybe being in the hospital around Christmas isn't so bad after all, I thought. My husband said that friends had brought meals to the family and offered to look after our four children. Outside my window, heavy snow was transforming our small town into a winter wonderland. *The kids have to be loving this*, I thought as I imagined them bundled in their snowsuits building a backyard snowman, or skating at Garfield School on the outdoor ice rink.

Would they include Adam, our handicapped son? I wondered. At age 5, he had just started walking independently, and I worried about him getting around on the ice and snow with his thin ankles. *Would anyone take him for a sled ride at the school?*

"More flowers!" The nurse's voice startled me from my thoughts as she came into the room carrying a beautiful centerpiece. She handed me the card while she made room for the bouquet among the poinsettias on the windowsill. "I guess we're going to have to send you home," she teased. "We're out of space here!"

"Okay with me," I agreed.

"Oh, I almost forgot these!" She took more cards from her pocket and put them on the tray. Before leaving the room, she pulled back the pale green privacy curtain between the two beds. While I was reading my get-well cards, I heard, "Yep, I like those flowers." I looked up to see the woman in the bed beside me push the curtain aside so she could see better. "Yep, I like your flowers," she repeated.

My roommate was a small forty-something woman with short, curly, gray hair who had Down's syndrome. Her hospital gown hung untied around her neck, and when she moved forward it exposed her bare back. I wanted to tie it for her, but I was still connected to an IV. She stared at my flowers with childlike wonder.

"I'm Bonnie," I told her. "What's your name?"

"Ginger," she said, rolling her eyes toward

the ceiling and pressing her lips together after she spoke. "Doc's gonna fix my foot. I'm gonna have suur-jeree tomorrow."

Ginger and I talked until dinner time. She told me about the group home where she lived and how she wanted to get back for her Christmas party. She never mentioned a family, and I didn't ask. Every few minutes she reminded me of her surgery scheduled for the next morning. "Doc's gonna fix my foot," she would say.

That evening I had several visitors, including my son Adam. Ginger chattered merrily to them, telling each about my pretty flowers. But mostly she kept an eye on Adam. And later, after everyone left, Ginger repeated over and over, just as she had about my flowers, "Yep, I like your Adam."

The next morning Ginger left for surgery, and the nurse came to help me take a short walk down the hall. It felt good to be on my feet. Soon I was back in our room. As I walked through the door, the stark contrast between the two sides of the room hit me. Ginger's bed stood neatly made, waiting for her return. But she had *no* cards, *no* flowers, and *no* visitors. My side bloomed with flowers, and the stack of get-well cards reminded me of just how much I was loved.

No one sent Ginger flowers or a card. In fact, no had called or visited her. *Is this what it will be like for Adam one day?* I wondered, then quickly put the thought from my mind.

I know, I decided. *I'll give her something of mine.*

I walked to the window and picked up the red-candled centerpiece with holly sprigs. *But this would look great on our Christmas dinner table*, I thought as I set the piece back down. *What about the poinsettias?* Then I realized how much the deep-red plants would brighten the entry of our turn-of-the-century home. *And of course, I can't give away Mom and Dad's roses, knowing we won't see them for Christmas this year*, I thought.

The justifications kept coming: *the flowers are beginning to wilt; this friend would be offended;*

I really could use this when I get home. I couldn't part with anything. Then I climbed back into my bed, placating my guilt with a decision to call the hospital gift shop and order Ginger some flowers of her own.

When Ginger returned from surgery, a candy striper brought her a small green Christmas wreath with a red bow. She hung it on the bare white wall above Ginger's bed. That evening I had more visitors, and even though Ginger was recuperating from surgery, she greeted each one and proudly showed them her Christmas wreath.

After breakfast the next morning, the nurse returned to tell Ginger that she was going home. "The van from the group home is on its way to pick you up," she said.

I knew Ginger's short stay meant she would be home in time for her Christmas party. I was happy for her, but I felt my own personal guilt when I remembered the hospital gift shop would not open for two more hours. Once more I looked around the room at my flowers. *Can I part with any of these?*

The nurse brought the wheelchair to Ginger's bedside. Ginger gathered her few personal belongings and pulled her coat from the hanger in the closet. "I've really enjoyed getting to know you, Ginger," I told her. My words were sincere, but I felt guilty for not following through on my good intentions.

The nurse helped Ginger with her coat and into the wheelchair. Then she removed the small wreath from the nail on the wall and handed it to Ginger. They turned toward the door to leave when Ginger said, "Wait!" Ginger stood up from her wheelchair and hobbled slowly to my bedside. She reached her right hand forward and gently laid the small wreath in my lap.

"Merry Christmas," she said. "You're a nice lady." Then she gave me a big hug.

"Thank you," I whispered. I couldn't say anything more as she hobbled back to the chair and headed out the door. I dropped my moist eyes to the small wreath in my hands. *Ginger's only gift,* I thought. *And she gave it to me.*

I looked toward her bed. Once again, her side of the room was bare and empty. But as I heard the "ping" of the elevator doors closing behind Ginger, I knew that she possessed much, much more than I.

BONNIE SHEPHERD

A Doll to Love

When I was in kindergarten, my teacher told us we were going to be able to bring a toy in to share with other children for Christmas. Well, in my little five-year-old mind, I thought, *Wow! I can bring in my Holly Hobbie doll!* I was thinking I would be sharing her with my classmates.

I was so attached to this doll. My mom had knitted a beautiful blanket for her, and I slept with her every night. I took care of her like a true mother would! You can imagine my hesitation when I took her to school that day, and my teacher told me to put her in the big toy bin in the hall. I figured we would all get a chance to play with the toys and then claim our own at the end of the day.

So I put Holly in the bin, not realizing I would never get to hold her again. I cried and cried that evening at home. I remember my mom trying to console me, but I was broken-hearted.

A few days later, as my mom was reading the newspaper, she called me to her, wanting to show me something. There on the front page was a little girl in the hospital with a serious illness, and in her arms was *my Holly Hobbie doll!* The article described the toy drive and how it brightened the lives of so many children at Christmastime. They had chosen my doll, my gift, however mistakenly given, to show the joy it brought that little girl.

I was so happy knowing my doll was with someone who would love her as much as I would. I was given the best gift of all that Christmas. The joy of giving is greater than I could ever receive.

HOPE SHICK

The manner of
giving is worth
more than the gift.

PIERRE CORNEILLE

It is more blessed to give than to receive.

THE BOOK OF ACTS

God Is Good

In 1978 I was living in the Chicago area with my four brothers, two sisters, and mom. We lived in a suburban home. We did not see our dad for a while. It was close to Christmas, and I knew that my mom's weekly check was not going to cover the bills, let alone give us a "Merry Christmas." We were all Christians and went to church. God had always supplied for our needs, but it was December 23, and being a seventeen-year-old I knew that that was when my mom usually started to prepare food for Christmas.

I also knew that our cupboards were bare. We all pitched in, but we were still short. I was a little bit concerned—after all, part of Christmas was a wonderful dinner of turkey, ham, and all the trimmings. So, I went into my mom's room and told her, "Mom, it is almost Christmas, and we do not have food for dinner." My mom said she was well aware of this and maybe God wanted us to just remember Him for what Christmas was all about.

I said yes, this could be, and it was okay for me. Then she said, "Let's you and I pray and see what God would want." So we did. I prayed very specifically for what I wanted and for His will to be done and left it with Him to the point that the next day came and I forgot about it.

Then at 7 P.M. came a knock at the door, and a delivery man from the local grocery store was there with a box of food. I looked in the box, but there was no turkey. I looked up and smiled and said thank-you, but he said, "Wait, there are six more boxes in the van!" And yes, there was a turkey, ham, and all the trimmings. Later that night I was throwing out the garbage when I found another frozen turkey on the back porch. God had provided for us above and beyond what we needed.

Ian Gliori

What can I give Him,

Poor as I am?

If I were a shepherd

I would bring a lamb,

If I were a wise man

I would do my part,

Yet what can I give Him,

Give my heart.

CHRISTINA ROSSETTI

Beating the Christmas Blues

The last thing I wanted to do the second Christmas after my divorce was put my five-year-old on a plane alone. But two days before the holiday, I loaded up our car and crept along snowy roads to the Portland, Oregon airport. Between tears, I told Heather to call me from her dad's home in Seattle. As I watched her plane disappear, I knew it wouldn't seem like Christmas without her.

Back home, I lay on the couch depressed, huddled under a mound of blankets. *It's just as well Heather's not here*, I thought, eyeing the stark room. Though my mom, dad, and Grandmother Ollie had traveled from eastern Oregon to spend the holiday with me, I hadn't put up a tree.

"Want to do some shopping today?" Mom asked. I shook my head, remembering all I had left in my purse for the month was $18. I hadn't even bought Heather a gift. "Patricia," she said, "I know you miss Heather, but I think getting out will make you feel better."

Following more nudges from Mom, we set out for the mall. I glanced at toys I might someday be able to buy for Heather, then sat down to wait for Mom and Grandma to finish their shopping. When we got back to the car, I realized I was almost out of gas, so I headed for the nearest station.

It was a raw evening, and the attendant, a teenaged boy in shirtsleeves, rushed about to serve his customers. As he darted from the cashier's stand to the cars, the boy slapped his gloved hands together. When we inched up, he asked through chattering teeth how much gas we needed. Before I could answer, Grandma started in.

"Young man," she asked, "where is your coat?"

"I don't have one," he said, smiling. "But don't worry about me. I'm doing a lot of running."

I handed the boy $5 for gas, and Grandma shook her head as he took the money. When we drove off, Grandma and Mom chattered on about the coatless teen. "What can we do?" I asked. "It's late," Mom said, "but maybe Fred Meyer's department store is still open. I bet we could get a nice coat there for that young man."

I turned around and sped back into town, whipping into Fred's parking lot 10 minutes before the store's closing. Inside, we tore through several coat racks. As we reached the last rack, Mom pulled out a green coat.

"This one's perfect!" she said. "It will keep him warmer than the others," Grandma echoed. With two minutes left till closing, Mom marched to the counter and pulled out $39. When she announced that we'd each have to pay $13 to split the bill, I gasped.

What was I thinking when I said I'd chip in? I wondered. *Thirteen dollars is all I have left!* Despite my panic, I fished the money from my purse and handed it over. Giving my last dime away didn't seem logical but it felt right.

Once in the car, we plotted how to give the present. Since I could move the fastest, Mom suggested that I jump out when we reached the station, hand the boy the coat, say "Jesus loves you!" and then leave.

When I handed the young man the coat and made my declaration, he looked puzzled. But before he could ask questions, I drove off. In the rearview mirror, I saw his mouth spread into a grin. He held the jacket in disbelief and looked into the distance at our car.

"You should see the look on his face!" said Mom, eyeing the boy through the rear window. "Well," Grandma said with a sigh, "that's one boy who won't freeze."

All the way home, the depression I had felt after Heather left slowly disappeared. As I hummed "Silent Night," the truth struck me: *While down in the dumps because my daughter was gone, I had forgotten what Christmas was about.*

PATRICIA HARBAUGH

*May you have the
greatest two gifts of all on
these holidays;
someone to love and
someone who loves you.*

JOHN SINOR

A Merry First Christmas

In May 1993, I became engaged to my now-husband Darryl. We were so looking forward to celebrating our first Christmas together as an "official" couple. But on the morning of December 24, I came down with a horrible case of the flu. By that afternoon, I was running a temperature of about 103 and went to bed.

My fiancé came over to check on me and asked if I wanted him to stay with me. I said no. Quite honestly, I just wanted to be left alone, and I thought he should go to his family's house to enjoy the celebration and pass out the gifts that I had bought for my soon-to-be in-laws.

Little did I know that his gift to me that year was a camcorder to videotape all our special events to come in the following years. He took the camcorder to his sister's house and recorded special get-well and Christmas wishes from all of my new family.

On Christmas morning I was feeling human again, and my temperature was back to normal. Darryl came over and first presented me with the camcorder, but he quickly put on the tape from the night before. Some of my new family had bought me gifts, and he had videoed them handing the camera a gift. He would then pause the tape and pull the gift out of the hall closet!

These sweet surprises made for a very merry first Christmas. It was the closest thing to celebrating Christmas with my new family under the circumstances. And now I have a permanent record of our first Christmas together.

ANNE BARTOLOTTI

And there were shepherds living out in the fields nearby, keeping watch over their flocks at night. An angel of the Lord appeared to them, and the glory of the Lord shone around them, and they were terrified. But the angel said to them, "Do not be afraid. I bring you good news of great joy that will be for all the people. Today in the town of David a Savior has been born to you; he is Christ the Lord. This will be a sign to you: You will find a baby wrapped in cloths and lying in a manger."

Suddenly a great company of the heavenly host appeared with the angel, praising God and saying, "Glory to God in the highest, and on earth peace to men on whom his favor rests."

When the angels had left them and gone into heaven, the shepherds said to one another, "Let's go to Bethlehem and see this thing that has happened, which the Lord has told us about." So they hurried off and found Mary and Joseph, and the baby, who was lying in the manger. When they had seen him, they spread the word concerning what had been told them about this child, and all who heard it were amazed at what the shepherds said to them.

THE BOOK OF LUKE

Thanks be to God for his indescribable gift!

THE BOOK OF 2 CORINTHIANS

The Christmas We Forgot Ourselves

Everything was as ready as it was going to get. It was Christmas Eve morning, and we were settling in to enjoy the day, when a call came from a woman we did not know. She had heard of a family with five teenagers, one of whom was in the hospital. The parents were out of work, and it didn't look much like Christmas at their home. The woman caller wanted to send an anonymous gift, so she dropped it off at our house with directions to the family's trailer.

Our girls, then about 8 and 11, thought it would be fun to add to the gift by gathering some of the goodies that had been arriving for our family and packing them up as presents. We decided to call three or four friends and ask them to bring whatever they could out of the excess that might be at their houses. Somehow, the real spirit of Christmas crept silently into the hearts of the contributors, and before long, people were braving the crowds and actually going shopping for new gifts for the teenagers.

Over the next two hours, at least 20 wrapped presents, whole hams, homemade cookies, and bags and bags of food, arrived at our house for the Christmas Eve delivery. Our little compact station wagon was so full, there was only room for a driver and one passenger.

When my husband arrived at the trailer, only one family member was at home; the others were visiting the hospital patient. The gifts filled their small living room. The one boy looked on in disbelief.

Looking back, none of us can remember what we got or gave each other that Christmas, but we all remember the year we forgot ourselves and made the day brighter for a family we never knew.

BONNY FANT

The greatest gift we can give one another is rapt attention to one another's existence.

SUE ATCHLEY EBAUGH

What child is this, who, laid to rest

On Mary's lap, is sleeping?

Whom angels greet with anthems sweet,

While shepherds watch are keeping?

This, this is Christ the King,

Whom shepherds guard and angels sing:

Haste, haste to bring Him laud,

The Babe, the Son of Mary!

So bring Him incense, gold, and myrrh,

Come peasant king to own Him,

The King of kings, salvation brings,

Let loving hearts enthrone Him.

Raise, raise the song on high,

The Virgin sings her lullaby:

Joy, joy, for Christ is born,

The Babe, the Son of Mary!

WILLIAM C. DIX
"What Child Is This?"

A Symbol of Faith

On Christmas Eve 1996, our family was ready to leave for church, but Taylor was still in his room. When I went downstairs I found him sitting on his bed with his Bible opened. He was struggling over the passage he was to read in the service that night.

"Mom, I really don't want to do this. They put my name on the program without asking me." His youth leader had assumed that being a pastor's son, Taylor would do fine reading Scripture in the program. At 14, Taylor's strengths were in music and art. He didn't mind being before the congregation singing or playing his drums in the band, but he dreaded reading out loud.

"Taylor," I told him, "if you don't feel you can do this, we can ask your youth leader to get someone else tonight."

"No, I'll do it this time, but never again."

That evening my husband, Roland, and I sat near the front of the church as three of our five children took part in the candlelight service. As Taylor stepped to the pulpit, the large white Moravian star that hung high at the front of the sanctuary rotated, catching my eye. The lighted star was hung every year from the first day of Advent to Epiphany. During Sunday worship service Taylor would often nudge me if the star turned when someone was speaking: it was as if God were nodding His approval.

As an artist, Taylor admired the three-dimensional star with its many points. He had learned to make a similar star out of folded paper and taught each member of our family. As a result, this year our Christmas tree held 200 tiny white paper stars that we had made together.

Standing tall in the pulpit, Taylor nervously cleared his throat and slowly began to read from Luke 2, where the angel appears to the shepherds: "Do not be afraid, I bring you good news of great joy that will be for all the people. Today in the town of David a Savior has been born to you; he is Christ the Lord."

Roland and I looked at each other as Taylor left the podium. We knew that God had helped our son face his fear and make it through the reading. After the service we found Taylor in the sanctuary putting out the candles. Walking out of the church, Roland told him, "When I saw you standing in the pulpit tonight, in the white robe with the gold cross around your neck, I knew whom you

belonged to and who would always take care of you."

When the phone rang the morning of December 27, the horrible news of the accident was more than we could comprehend. Taylor and his cousin, Shep, had been working to pull a piece of farm machinery called a Bobcat out of the mud at my brother's place. The tractor Taylor was driving flipped back over on him, killing him instantly.

News of Taylor's death stunned our church community, and word spread quickly. Soon our home was filled with family and friends. The presence of friends who also had experienced the death of a child helped strengthen my faith.

At Taylor's memorial service we chose to celebrate his life, not focus on his death. He had not been a perfect child, but God had made him perfect now. When I sat down in the sanctuary with almost 1,500 people, I felt at peace; I had never before felt so much love.

At the end of the service, Roland and I, along with our daughters—Christin, Mary, Sarah, and Rebecca—went to the altar to light our candles. Because the last thing Taylor had done at the church was put out the candles, it seemed fitting that we relight all the candles in memory of him.

I had two choices. I could close myself off from others and live a life of sadness and gloom, or I could live life to the fullest and remember that every day I can experience Christmas. I chose to live life. That is what Taylor would have wanted me to do.

A teacher at Taylor's school called and asked if I could come to talk to some of Taylor's friends. For many of them, this was the first death they had experienced and they were having a tough time making sense of it all. At home, we had given stars from our tree to our grieving friends. I asked if he minded if I brought materials to teach the students how to make paper stars while we talked about our grief. He agreed.

We called our time together "good grief" as we created stars out of paper and talked about faith and trust in God.

Everywhere our family went we would see stars hanging from rearview mirrors. We felt connected to Taylor and to his friends. But most of all, we could see that God was reaching others through Taylor's short life.

At church that Sunday after Christmas, the star at the front of the sanctuary was the only remaining symbol of the holiday. Taylor was right. It had been the last time he would read before the congregation, but those words he read made all the difference: "Do not be afraid. I bring you good news of great joy that will be for all the people. Today in the town of David a Savior has been born to you; he is Christ the Lord."

After receiving Communion, I looked up at the star. It turned halfway around, then back and stopped. I thought of Taylor standing there only a few days earlier. This time it seemed as if Taylor was nudging me from heaven saying, "Everything is okay, Mom."

EMILIE BARNHARDT

Every good and perfect gift

is from above,

coming down from the

Father of the heavenly lights...

THE BOOK OF JAMES

A New Christmas Tradition

For years, Christmas day had been the same for my children and me: opening gifts, attending church, and eating too much food. But one year I wanted something more. I read that a local church needed volunteers to help serve Christmas dinner to the needy. I had done the same thing 20 years earlier and decided to give my kids the chance to serve as I had.

Christmas arrived, and soon the hall was filled with hundreds of volunteers. Someone said a prayer into a microphone while the rest of us joined hands around the room. Then the serving line began. We filled foam take-out containers with food and packed them into cartons to be delivered to the homes. Drivers were in short supply, so I volunteered for the job.

The Rhode Island streets were icy as we drove to our stops. My children (ages 10, 8, and 6) took turns walking up to the houses with me to deliver the food.

One beautiful elderly woman using a walker greeted us at the door. Her unhappy face mustered a smile. Next, we visited an older colonial home with beds arranged in the living room. The youngest, most able-bodied resident—he was about 90—cared for the other five men.

We went to a run-down apartment occupied by a just-turned-senior citizen on oxygen. The man's relative thanked us and showed us out, remarking on the damage years of smoking had caused. Another house was so dilapidated, I wondered whether somebody actually lived there. But the "Mister" of the "Mr. and Mrs." answered the bell and gave a somber and respectful "thank you" before retreating to a dark parlor. Another man answered the door wearing an undershirt and mumbled "Merry Christmas" over his TV blasting in the background. A mother holding a disheveled three-year-old thanked us profusely, as though she hadn't seen food like this for a long time.

The sun reflected off the ice as we pulled away from our last stop. My children and I talked about lots of things—white hair, old age, wisdom, and the importance of taking care of the body. I challenged my own bias against welfare recipients.

Soon we were headed for home. Our tasty food and warm home were surpassed only by the warmth we felt from inside: not of accomplishment but of gratitude for being able to serve; not of the meaning of Christmas alone, but of the meaning of Christianity as well.

For me, it was about allowing the Spirit to conquer my intransigent nature. For my kids, it was about awakening to the needs of others. For all of us, it was a Christmas we would never forget.

STEVE SULLIVAN

Giving presents is a talent;
to know what a person wants,
to know when and how to get it,
to give it lovingly and well.

PAMELA GLENCONNER

A Charming Christmas Memory

I grew up as one of eight children, living with my mom and dad in a small Ohio town. After the first week of December, the local college went on Christmas break, which was a kind of signal for my sisters, brothers, and me. My parents would drive us through town, and we would select our family tree from the ones prematurely pitched out on the sidewalks by students from the dormitories. I can still see the pines and spruces leaning against the trashcans, the used tinsel glistening in the sun. Year after year, the throwaway tree we selected became the center of our family festivities.

One Christmas morning is fixed in my memory. Our family was seated around the secondhand tree, which that year occupied more than half our living room. A crooked star was perched on top, where the tree had been cut to clear our low ceiling. Dad assumed his role of announcing the names on the packages and then passing them out. Some were so large they had to be pushed across the linoleum floor.

It was always an exciting moment, but this year the thrill of what was in store for me was dashed when I did not hear my name. Ignored in the activity, I watched my brothers and sisters as they ripped the wrapping from their boxes. I bit my lip to hold back the tears. Then Dad saw another present under the tree. "Looks like we forgot one here," he said, as he handed me an unusually small package.

What? That's all? I thought, as he laid the box on the palm of my hand. It was so tiny that the label with my name on it stuck over the side. I blinked my eyes in disappointment as I remembered how tight money was in our family, especially this year when the house needed repairs.

The wrapping paper came off, and a white box now shook in my hand as I lifted the lid and gazed inside. There on a flat square of cotton was the most beautiful silver charm bracelet I had ever seen. A heavy chain that fit exactly around my wrist held two glistening charms—an angel and a heart that said, "I love you."

I could not talk. I had wanted a charm

bracelet like those of the other girls at school, but I thought we could never afford one. As my mother reached over to help me fasten the latch, I threw my arms around both my parents: "Thank you! Oh, Daddy and Mommy, thank you!"

I can't remember what the others got that Christmas morning. But I can still see the sunlight reflecting off my long-awaited charm bracelet as it dangled delicately from my wrist.

I have opened other "little boxes" throughout my life to find big truths inside— all of which I needed and some of which I had wanted for a long time. These presents have come unexpectedly, when God has spoken through the ordinary, often difficult events in my life.

LYNDA HUNTER

What brings joy
to the heart is
not so much the
friend's gift as
the friend's love.

SAINT ALFRED OF
RIEVAULX

A Season for Angels

It had been a tough year, moving to a new and expensive area—small town to big city. We were trying to adjust, making new friends, and finding it difficult to make ends meet.

Our family of five joined a wonderful church right away. It was made up of fifty loving families, the smallest church in the area. We were able to get involved immediately and met true brothers and sisters in Christ.

Because of our move we were without money even for groceries. One evening a Christmas Angel took me grocery shopping. Meanwhile two other blessed Christmas Angels (all women from our church) brought in a huge, live Christmas tree and set it up (decorations and all), and brought Christmas gifts for our entire family.

When I arrived home I was greeted with a festive house full of Christmas cheer and Christ's love. They then gave us money to drive home to Arizona to be with my husband's family. The look on his mother's face when we drove up Christmas morning reflected the feelings I had in my heart for our Christmas Angels! I'll never forget this Christmas because it held for us the true meaning of what our Christian family is about.

YUKI JOHNSON

One of the
great joys of
Christmastime is
giving presents to
those you love.

SANDRA BOYNTON
Christmastime

The Faith of a Child

It was a rainy morning that holiday season as I sat at home working at my desk. I was deep in thought when I felt a small hand on my shoulder. My son, Jason, just 4 years old, had walked in and waited quietly for me to stop writing so he could talk to me.

As I turned and met his eyes, he communicated a sense of purpose that I hadn't felt from him before. "Daddy, I want a bicycle for Christmas," he announced.

I was afraid of that. Three years earlier I had left a well-paying job to join a small ministry outreach to those living on the Mexican border near San Diego.

Although my wife, Sherry, and I were certain of God's call, we struggled financially. We had no savings, no credit (except in the bank of heaven), and no money for Christmas presents for our two children. And now my son tells me he wants a bicycle! How could I look into his piercing, trusting, expectant eyes and say, "I'm sorry, Son, but we don't have any money"?

I placed my hands on his shoulders and said, "Jason, I'm sure God would love for you to have a bicycle. I'm also sure He wants you to know you can trust Him. In order for you to know that your Christmas bicycle is especially for you from Jesus, let's tell Him what color bike you want."

"Okay…I want a green bike."

We began praying every day and every night for that special green bike. We waited to see how the Lord would work out this object-lesson for Jason—and for Sherry and me. But a week before Christmas, we still had no money and no green bike. My faith began to waiver.

Then my friend Paul called. "Would Jason like a bicycle for Christmas?" he asked. Paul was calling from a garage sale where he'd found a bike in great shape. "It's got trainer wheels, and it'll fit him perfectly."

I could hardly contain my excitement until I remembered something. "Paul, can you tell me what color the bike is?"

"Sure. It's yellow."

I didn't say anything for a long time. "Is something wrong?" he asked. "Yeah, Paul, this is going to sound crazy but the bike's the wrong color."

Now it was his turn to be silent.

"You see, we've been praying for a green bike."

"Oh, I understand."

Now my own lack of faith kicked in. Christmas is only a week away. *Jason won't remember we had been praying for a green bike. He'd still know God had been faithful. Wouldn't he?*

"Paul, why don't you go ahead and get the bike anyway."

That afternoon Sherry and Jason walked by some bicycles in a local department store. Jason stopped and stared. "Mommmy!" he jumped and pointed. "I want that bike!"

Sherry was taken back. "Jason, honey, that's not a green bike. Haven't we been telling Jesus you want a green one?"

"No, Mommy, I want that one. I want a yellow bike!"

That night, as we tucked Jason into bed, we marveled at God's faithfulness. But the topper came when Jason bowed his head and asked the Lord not to get confused by his request for a green bike. "I really want a yellow one!" he exclaimed.

That Christmas, we knew the Lord had already heard him, loud and clear.

RICK GREGORY

The magi, as you know, were wise men— wonderfully wise men— who brought gifts to the Babe in the manger. They invented the art of giving Christmas presents.

O. HENRY
The Gift of the Magi

For to us a child is born,

to us a son is given....

And he will be called

Wonderful Counselor, Mighty God,

Everlasting Father, Prince of Peace.

THE BOOK OF ISAIAH

It came upon the midnight clear,

That glorious song of old,

From angels bending near the earth

To touch their harps of gold!

"Peace on the earth, good will to men,

From heaven's all gracious King!"

The world in solemn stillness lay

To hear the angels sing.

EDMUND H. SEARS

"It Came Upon A Midnight Clear"

The Centerpiece

I had just come home from my first semester of college, and like nearly everyone else, I spent the days preceding December 25 going through the motions, the holiday equivalent of brushing my teeth. I did the expected: Buying presents, singing songs, and looking at the residential light displays—including the crèche with the shepherds gathered around the Christ child while Santa watched approvingly from the roof. Now it was Christmas Day—the cymbal clash at the end of the drum roll. *But where was the magic?*

Certainly not in the weather. Like most Christmases in Oregon, it was one of those in-between days—too cold to be pleasant, too warm to snow. It was one of those drab days where you wanted the weather to do something, to suddenly muster itself into a driving rainstorm or break into soul-cleansing sunshine. But it would not.

As my parents, sister, and I made our way north to my uncle's house, the clouds hung low over the Coast Range and, like my own overcast mood, showed no signs of clearing. White Christmases, I had decided, were reserved for schmaltzy Jimmy Stewart movies and Kodak commercials in which everybody was so busy smiling and hugging and spreading holiday cheer that they didn't stop to consider what the celebration was really all about.

I knew that 2,000 years ago shepherds had seen an angel and heard a message of the Messiah, of healing, and of hope. But as we drove along, it all seemed so far away—not 2,000 years away, but light-years away. I looked at the houses as we drove by, imagining families eating dinner and opening presents and watching football on TV. *But where was the message?*

Certainly not in our 20th-century celebrations. On this day, the sign in the sky was not a star, but the smokestack of a paper plant. We always drove by the paper plant en route to my uncle's house, and Christmas Day was the one day of the year when it was shut down. That was our sign that a child had been born. Rejoice, for unto freeway travelers is given a day without smoke.

We arrived at my uncle's house, four more people in a mix of diversity—linked not by common interests or values, but by blood. I had once felt keenly part of this clan, as if

returning each year was like putting on a pair of well-worn tennis shoes that fit just right. This year, I felt no such comfort. Perhaps it was my age. At 18, I was too young to believe in children's laughter, too collegiate to be engrossed in the Christmas story, too confused to be anything other than the holiday cynic.

This was my year of questioning—the year I wanted to quit college, stop writing and become a milkman; the year my faith had been battered by so many professors and live-for-today dorm neighbors that I had nearly believed it was easier to switch than fight. *But where was the meaning?*

Certainly not in this room of people, I thought, as I half-listened to the small talk. They were good folks, but it was all so programmed. The same people, the same

menu we ate every year, and then we all joked about how much we'd overeaten.

Then it happened. As we readied to open our Christmas presents—the last stop on this train ride of tradition—Uncle Bill stood up and announced he had something he wanted to share. Everyone exchanged puzzled looks. This wasn't part of the script.

My uncle looked around the room. He said he had been thinking, and he had decided it was important to remember *why* we celebrate Christmas. He wanted to read something to help remind us, he said. I figured he would read Luke 2—that's the safe thing—but he didn't. Instead he began reciting a poem written by an anonymous author, a piece called "One Solitary Life."

Here is a man who was born of Jewish parents,
the child of a peasant woman…
He never wrote a book.
He never held an office.
He never owned a home.
He never had a family.
He never went to college.
He never put a foot inside a big city.
He never traveled two hundred miles
from the place he was born.
He never did one of the things that
usually accompany greatness.
He had no credentials but himself…

The two dozen people in the living room remained still. Nobody even whispered. We all

house, the same conversations and the same instrumental guitar music coming softly from the stereo.

It was all warm and comfortable and cozy. We seemingly had it all—and yet it left me empty, as if something were missing. We ate turkey and mashed potatoes and Aunt Ruth's green Jell-O with marshmallows, the same just looked straight ahead as Uncle Bill continued, realizing that we were in the midst of something strangely special.

While still a young man, the tide of popular
opinion turned against him.
His friends ran away. One of them denied him…
He was nailed to a cross between two thieves.
His executioners gambled for
the only piece of property
he had on earth…his coat.
When he was dead, he was taken down
and laid in a borrowed grave,
through the pity of a friend.

My uncle's eyes grew misty. So did some others—and so did mine.

Nineteen wide centuries have come and gone,
and he is the centerpiece of the human race
and the leader of the column of progress.
I am far within the mark when I say
that all the armies that ever marched,
and all the navies that were ever built,…
have not affected the life of man upon earth
as powerfully as has that One Solitary Life.

Had this been the movies, flakes of snow would have begun to fall outside. But snow did not fall. Nor did a star appear in the sky. Instead, Uncle Bill simply sat down. Slowly, people resumed their small talk as they began opening presents.

I don't know how the reading affected others, but for me, it was more than a temporary cease-fire for my inner turmoil. The poem was light for my darkness of doubt. It bonded me once again with the relatives whom I had allowed seem so distant, because I was reminded that One Solitary Life had been given as a gift to each one of us, whether we accept it or not.

It was the reassurance that the child of that peasant woman had grown into humankind's only hope. It was a reminder that, amid the routine, what had been missing on this Christmas Day was not snow on the ground or a star in the sky. What had been missing—both on this day and in my life—was the guest of honor, the centerpiece of the celebration.

BOB WELCH

Are you willing to believe that

love is the strongest thing in the

world—stronger than death—

and that the blessed life which

began in Bethlehem nineteen

hundred years ago is the image

and brightness of the Eternal

Love? Then you can keep

Christmas, and if you keep it for

a day, why not always?

HENRY VAN DYKE

"Keeping Christmas"